DISCARDED BY

JO+

1057-91

MW01179112

HARBOUR
LIGHTS
BURLINGTON BAY

(Ontario Archives)

# HARBOUR LIGHTS
## BURLINGTON BAY

Mary Weeks-Mifflin & Ray Mifflin

THE BOSTON MILLS PRESS

CANADIAN CATALOGUING IN PUBLICATION DATA

Weeks-Mifflin, Mary, 1951-
  Harbour lights: the story of Burlington Bay

Bibliography: p.
Includes index.
ISBN 0-919783-75-9

1. Harbours - Ontario - Hamilton Harbour.
2. Hamilton Harbour (Ont.) - Navigation.
I. Mifflin, Ray, 1950-   . II. Title.

HE554.H34W43 1988    ~~386.80971352~~   C88-095300-4

971.35
Wee

© Mary Weeks-Mifflin & Ray Mifflin, 1989

Published by:
THE BOSTON MILLS PRESS
132 Main Street
Erin, Ontario N0B 1T0
TEL: (519) 833-2407
FAX: (519) 833-2195

American Association
for State and Local History
Award of Merit

Winners of the
Heritage Canada
Communications Award

Design by John Denison
Cover design by Gill Stead
Typeset by Speed River Graphics, Guelph
Printed by Ampersand, Guelph

The Publisher wishes to acknowledge the financial
assistance and encouragement of The Canada
Council, the Ontario Arts Council and the Office of
the Secretary of State.

JOHN T. TUCK SCHOOL

*This is the story of a canal, a lighthouse,
and early navigation into the harbour
known as Burlington Bay, at the
western end of Lake Ontario.*

# ACKNOWLEDGEMENTS

Many individuals, societies and government agencies have made important contributions to this book. We wish to say thank you.

Peter Coletti and "family" — Your fascinating stories, pictures, and friendship are greatly valued. Thanks for the many delightful hours spent clambering around "your" lighthouse.

Roger Chapman — Thanks for your cheerful enthusiasm, your photographic talents, and your continual support.

Gerry Ouderkirk — Special thanks for your many hours of research on Lake Ontario shipping. It has been very enjoyable exchanging material with a fellow "Greendale graduate."

Hamilton Public Library, Special Collection — Your research facilities and picture collections are excellent.

Joseph Brant Museum — Special thanks to Barbara Featero and Ann Urquhart.

Public Archives Canada — The following staff deserve recognition for their indispensable efforts: Richard Brown, Ed Atkinson and Brian Brothman, Marine Division; Lise Ruchert and Sharon Uno, Photographic Services; Diane Paquette, Map and Chart Collection.

Ontario Archives — Your Research Department was extensive and informative, and Ken McPherson in the Photographic Division could never do enough for us.

Toronto Marine Historical Society — Thanks to the membership, who welcomed us into their organization and supplied invaluable pictures and information on Great Lakes shipping. Special thanks to John H. Bascom, Jay Bascom, Lorne Joyce and Dyke Cobb.

Canadian Coast Guard, Prescott, Ontario — Thanks to Cal Drake, Hughie Jones and Ted Cater for your patience, pictures and help. It was greatly appreciated.

Canadian Coast Guard, Toronto, Ontario — Thanks to John Whitaker and Alfie Yip for your help and support in our past, present and future endeavours.

Canadian Coast Guard, Parry Sound, Ontario — Special thanks to Captain J. Kennedy, Captain W. Sadler, Edmund Lee, Randy Childerhouse and Sharon Heidman for playing an important part in our research on Canadian lighthouses.

Burlington Historical Society — Thanks to

Mary Fraser for her years of work transcribing the lightkeeper's diary of George Thompson, and to the Society's membership, who really care about our local history.

Ivan Brooks, Ron Beaupre, Ester Summers, Aileen Love, Mary Wright and Mike Gushulak — Thanks for graciously opening up your homes and sharing pictures and information, and offering encouragement.

Special thanks to Walter Lewis and Peter Warwick for well-researched information on early shipbuilding in the Head of the Lakes region.

McMaster University, Mills Memorial Library, Documents Room — Thanks for your excellent research facilities.

Canadian Centre for Inland Waters and Hydrographic Services.

Burlington Spectator, Marg Langton and John Gast — Thank you for taking an interest in our work and following our progress.

Duncan and Wright Cameras — Your special attention to our photographic needs was greatly appreciated.

Elaine Weeks, a dear friend and sister-in-law — You're the greatest typist anyone could ask for.

Thanks to our family and friends who have stood behind us and supported a pair of "lighthouse nuts."

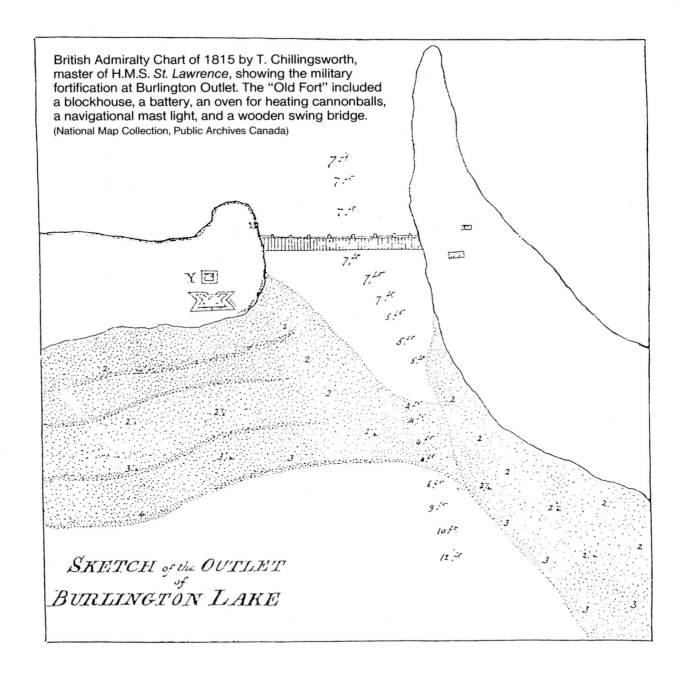

British Admiralty Chart of 1815 by T. Chillingsworth, master of H.M.S. *St. Lawrence*, showing the military fortification at Burlington Outlet. The "Old Fort" included a blockhouse, a battery, an oven for heating cannonballs, a navigational mast light, and a wooden swing bridge. (National Map Collection, Public Archives Canada)

SKETCH of the OUTLET of BURLINGTON LAKE

# IN THE BEGINNING

A nor'easter was blowing, the seas were rising, and the British flagship *Wolf* was struggling, her top main mast sheared off. The year was 1813 and Chauncey's American squadron was in pursuit. The "Burlington Races" had begun.

British commander Sir James Heo signalled to the corvette *Royal George*, the brigantine *Prince Regent*, and the trio of schooners which followed, that they were heading for refuge at Burlington Bay, even though it was landlocked by a long, sandy beach. Only a shallow creek, known locally as the "Outlet," provided any entrance to the harbour, and there was a great risk that the 426-ton *Wolf* would be driven ashore.

Oddly enough, it was the gale that saved them. It had piled up the waters at the head of Lake Ontario and scoured a passage through the bar, allowing the squadron access. The American fleet chose to break off pursuit and head for the safety of Fort George, since a reconnaissance party in July of that year had revealed the shallowness of the Outlet.

The British had been lucky and they knew it. Had the engagement lasted a few hours longer, only the seaman's lantern hoisted on the flagpole by the blockhouse at the Outlet would have provided any aid for Heo's young navigator, Richardson. It also proved to them that a proper harbour entrance and lighthouse were necessary before the head of the lakes region could be opened up for commerce.

Burlington Bay had always held promise. Christened Little Lake on early charts, it possessed many of the qualities of an excellent harbour: good anchorage, adequate protection, and an easily defensible position. Unfortunately it had one major drawback: limited access.

To solve this problem the construction of a canal was planned, and to an untrained observer this would seem a simple task — all that was required was a channel through a sandy beach — but it was a project besieged with problems from the start.

To begin with, following the War of 1812, control of the Outlet fell into the hands of two very influential families, the Brants and the Chisholms. John Brant was leader of the Indian armies and his neighbour, George Chisholm, was a staunch Tory, Area Magistrate and Roads Commissioner.

They set up a forwarding trade at the Outlet, taking advantage of the fact that fully loaded schooners could not navigate the harbour entrance. Warehouses were built, and goods from Dundas and Hamilton were sailed or rowed to the Outlet. They were then transferred onto schooners anchored in Lake Ontario. George Chisholm's son John was appointed Customs Collector at the Outlet, while another son, William, began a shipbuilding business on the north neck of the beach, hiring master shipwright Jacob Randall and sons to craft the schooners *Mohawk Chief*, *Rebecca and Eliza*, *General Brock* and *Telegraph*. This fleet of vessels listed Burlington Bay as their home port and were commanded respectively by Daniel Campbell, Edward Zealand, William Kerr, and Philo Bates. These schooners traded between the Outlet and Prescott, Ontario.

At this same shipyard Jacob Randall and his sons built the schooner *Union*, which was 150 tons and was described by the *Niagara Gleaner* of July 19, 1824, as "the largest and finest Merchant vessel on the lake, now, or perhaps ever was."

A week later, with Captain John Moshier at the wheel, the *Union* capsized in the St. Lawrence two miles above Brockville. Three children in the hold were drowned.

At the Outlet, John Chisholm continued the maintenance of the mast light at the blockhouse, but it failed to aid the schooner *Union* the following year when, according to the *Niagara Gleaner* of September 24, 1825, it went aground near Burlington Outlet. The owners were so upset they decided to convert her into a steamboat the following year. Known as the *Niagara*, she went on to become the most unprofitable, slow, and ill-fitted steamboat on the Great Lakes.

Due to thriving forwarding and shipbuilding businesses, and the influence of the Brant and Chisholm families, the government was forced to choose a site 100 yards south of the Outlet for their canal. It became the first public work contracted for in the newly formed Upper Canada.

On March 19, 1823, the government was authorized to obtain a loan of £5,000 sterling to begin construction of a canal in the District of Gore between Burlington Bay and Lake Ontario. Interest on the loan was to be paid for by tolls collected on goods and vessels. William Chisholm and William Kerr (brother-in-law of John Brant) were two of the commissioners appointed to oversee construction. These two families were determined to retain control of the harbour entrance.

Francis Hall was appointed engineer of the canal works, having recently completed the plans for Brock's Monument. His original scroll design dated September 13, 1824, called for a canal 72 feet wide, complete with piers lining both sides and a protective breakwater on the Lake Ontario side. This wedge-shaped breakwater was designed to keep sand out of the mouth of the channel and to house the first "permanent" lighthouse at Burlington Bay. Rather than a warning of dangerous shoals, this lighthouse was to be a guiding beacon for the canal entrance. To avoid confusion, the mast-head light at the Outlet was discontinued.

James Gordon Strowbridge from the Solon

One of the earliest Canadian schooners to sail Lake Ontario was the *Britannia*.
She was built in 1821 by Amos S. Roberts and was owned for a time by William
Chisholm, the founder of Oakville. (Mr. Roberts also repaired the schooner *Euretta*
and renamed her the *Jane of Burlington Bay* in 1823.) (Joseph Brant Museum)

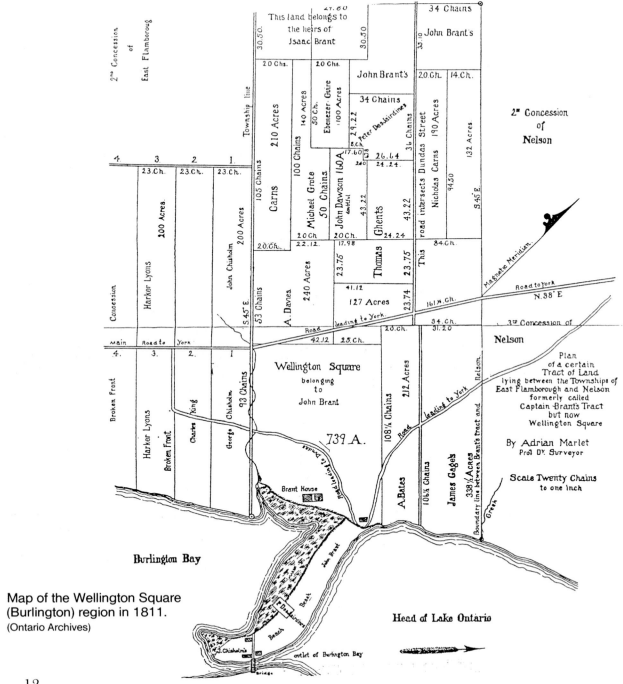

Map of the Wellington Square
(Burlington) region in 1811.
(Ontario Archives)

12

The Temperance Inn was originally built in 1840 by Philo Bates, master of the schooner *Telegraph* of Burlington Bay. (Joseph Brant Museum)

JOHN T. TUCK SCHOOL

Courtland Co. of New York was hired as contractor. Work began with a dozen men using shovels and wheelbarrows to dig a trench 40 feet wide across the beach. This continued until water level was reached and then a horse-powered dredge was employed to scoop endless buckets of sand onto a scow that in turn dumped the sand back into the lake. Strowbridge used horse power until the fall of 1825, when it became obvious that a more powerful steam dredge was needed to complete the contract.

The level of the lakes could only support one proper channel, and constant dredging was required even to maintain a minimum 10-foot depth. Wooden piers filled with stone were constructed to line the canal, stone being brought from Hamilton mountain at $3 a cord. As well, a watch house for sheltering sailors was constructed on the south pier.

By the summer of 1826 work had progressed sufficiently to allow passage of vessels drawing less than 10 feet of water, and on June 4, 1826, a race was organized between three crack schooners to compete for the honour of being the first ship to enter the canal. Captain Edward Zealand, commanding the *Rebecca and Eliza*, was the first to navigate the channel and triumphantly anchored off Port Hamilton.

A typical early mast light. The lanterns were hoisted up flagpoles or masts to provide temporary aid for mariners. The range of these lanterns was limited even with built-in lenses. (Canadian Coast Guard, Prescott)

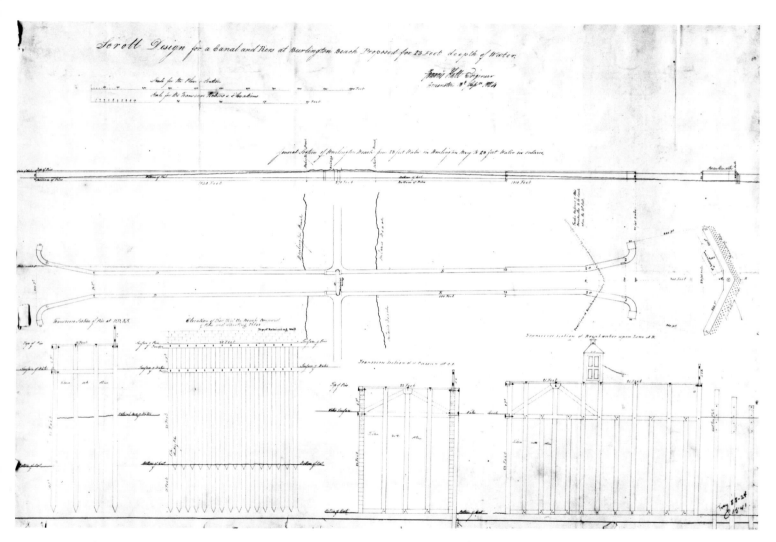

Original scroll design for the Burlington Bay Ship Canal
dated September 13, 1824. Engineer Francis Hall also
designed Brock's Monument.

(National Map Collection, Public Archives Canada)

The grand opening of the Burlington Bay Canal was scheduled for July 1, 1826. Unfortunately the opening of the canal brought about its first closure.

Lieutenant-Governor Sir Peregrine Maitland, complete with retinue and a military band, was scheduled to sail through the canal in William Chisholm's 60-ton schooner, the *General Brock*, heading a small fleet of vessels. Militia were to line the banks of the canal and fire a salute. However, as the *General Brock* rounded the lighthouse at the breakwater entrance, the schooner was hit by a cross breeze, swung around in the channel, grounded and effectively blocked the canal. Lines were thrown to Strowbridge and his men, but the vessel held fast and, in the confusion, one of the band members fell overboard and was drowned. The Lieutenant-Governor was forced to transfer to a six-oared barge. With the Union Jack flying at the mast, he rowed through the canal to open it. Needless to say, government officials were not impressed with the way the contract had been carried out and demanded that the canal be widened to its original 72-foot clearance and deepened to 12 feet.

In the ensuing months Strowbridge ran into financial difficulties, since the government would not pay him for the original work done, and was frequently arrested for debts. As a result he was prevented from superintending the works for long periods of time. Subcontractors took over, because even when out on bail Strowbridge could not go beyond the gaol (jail) limits. He would put one foot over Wellington Street to show contempt for the ruling, but that was as far as he dared go.

A series of gales during the winter of 1829-30 spelled disaster for Burlington Bay Canal's first contractor. The entrance breakwater and lighthouse were destroyed and the piers on the Lake Ontario side were swept away. A huge sand bar 40 feet in width was formed 300 feet from shore, over which there was only 6½ feet of water.

Nine vessels wintering in the bay, including the schooner *George Canning*, were trapped by the bar. Ironically the *George Canning* had been driven out of the Niagara River by ice earlier the same winter and, unable to enter York harbour, would have been lost with all crew aboard had the canal not been open.

The government took immediate steps to clear the sand bar and repair the damage. New piers were laid down by Captain Mann and Jacob Spaun. Stone for the piers was raised from the lake bed. Working in water up to their waists, crews used long iron bars to free the stone and then loaded it on scows. In deeper water, long-handled two-prong rakes were employed, and sometimes even larger rakes and derricks were necessary. Once the scow was loaded, the cargo was transferred to an awaiting schooner and taken to the piers.

Both the crews and schooners soon became known as "stonehookers." However, it was felt that stonehooking accelerated soil erosion, and it was not uncommon for these crews to be

Schooner and scow "stonehooking." (Ontario Archives)

John Chisholm, first collector of tolls and customs at Burlington Bay Canal.
(Oakville Historical Society)

greeted with shotgun blasts from angry beachfront residents. Mariners involved in "hooking" at the canal in 1830 included John Hart, Freeman Bray, Nehemiah Corey, H. Brown, Collins, Stanton and McDonald.

Another government improvement to the canal was the construction of a 62-foot swing bridge on an iron pivot. The bridge was put into use on October 1, 1830, replacing the four floating bridges and winter bridges employed since 1826. This lasted until the schooner *Elsie Hope*, under Captain McKay, dismounted the bridge before it could be swung.

Mooring posts or bollards were laid down for vessels outside the south pier in Burlington Bay. As well, on November 14, 1832, the Burlington Bay commissioners were pleased to announce that two new mast lights had been constructed to guide vessels to the harbour entrance.

Appropriations were made for maintaining the lights and attending the bridge. The "lighthouse" was placed under the direction of the Collector of Tolls, John Chisholm. Chisholm immediately hired M. Homer to attend the lights. He was paid five shillings a day and became the first recorded lighthouse keeper on the beach.

A few other personalities living at the beach in the early 1830s were as follows:

Colonel William Chisholm continued to maintain a presence at the canal by establishing a large general merchandise store north of the canal, even though he moved his shipbuilding industry to 16 Mile Creek, where he became Collector of Customs opened the harbour and became the founder of Oakville.

Captain Willet Green Miller lived at the canal and was a master shipwright who, over the years, built or helped build a score of sailing vessels. At the age of 16, young Miller had been reprimanded for a misdemeanor while serving as an American naval cadet and ran away to sea. Stowing aboard a schooner bound for Hamilton, Willet Miller found himself shipwrecked on Burlington Beach when gale-force winds drove the vessel ashore in 1824.

Willet Miller became an apprentice in the shipbuilding trade and gradually rose to a partnership in the firm of Bante and Miller. At Burlington Beach shipyards Willet Miller helped craft the schooners *Union*, *Rebecca and Eliza*, *Telegraph*, *Trafalgar*, *General Brock*, *Ann of Hamilton*, *Ann and Susan*, *Highland Chief* and *Farmer's Daughter*. As well, Willet Miller helped rebuild the *Clara C.* of Genesee, which had run aground on Burlington beach in 1832.

Captain Miller not only built ships but also sailed the lakes in command of the *Phoenix* and the *Wheeler*. He found the climate at the head of the lakes favourable and lived to 100 years of age.

Captain Edward Zealand lived on the beach at this time and commanded a series of vessels on the Great Lakes. His son, also named Edward, had the distinction of being commander of his own vessel at the young age of 12.

Philip McGee kept a tavern called the Ship's Inn at the canal. Philip also ran the ferry and, being a shoemaker by trade, set up a small stall in the corner of the ferry scow. Since sand, water and leather don't mix, he soon earned enough to have the schooner *Daniel O'Connell* built for him on the beach. He ended his days frozen to death on the bay while walking home from church.

Job Lodor of Ancaster kept store on the south side of the piers. He had a stock of general merchandise and commissioned the building of a steamboat on the beach. Local reports claim the steamboat was christened the *Chief Justice Robinson* in 1831 and was subsequently sold to E. Browne of Hamilton, who converted it into a three-masted schooner called the *Grampus*.

At this time the beach and canal area were almost entirely inhabited by fishermen, mariners, wholesalers and tavern keepers, and when the dreaded ship's sickness cholera struck in 1832, many inhabitants perished.

Dr. Daniel Black was appointed health inspector for all vessels carrying immigrants into Burlington Bay and a quarantine station was set up on the beach. Dr. Black himself died of cholera on August 13, 1832.

Seven gales struck the beach from the time tolls were first collected in 1828 until the end of 1832, but it was a late October gale in 1831 which impressed upon the residents at the head of the lake that a proper lighthouse was still very necessary.

The schooner *Commerce*, from Oswego, New

In 1837 a 54-foot octagonal wooden lighthouse was built at the canal. It was similar in design to the main light at Port Dalhousie, pictured here. (Courtesy of Roger Chapman)

York, was driven aground on Burlington Beach opposite the farm of William Lottridge with a full cargo of salt and merchandise belonging to merchants of Hamilton and Dundas. The salt and merchandise were totally destroyed. Cries for a lighthouse to mark the treacherous entrance to the piers were voiced by Captain Lucas and area residents. These cries were repeated in 1836 when the schooner *Elizabeth* went ashore on the north shore of the lake and had to be pulled off by the steamer *Gildersleeve* and towed to the canal. Rumours that "wreckers" were using false lights on the beach to lure vessels aground made the construction of a lighthouse of vital importance.

It was not until 1837 that a 54-foot wooden lighthouse (from base to vane) was finally built at the canal by John L. Williams, an American. It was a frame octagonal-shaped structure, clapboarded, and set on a stone foundation. It was similar in design to the main lighthouse at Port Dalhousie.

During 1837 £12 19s was collected in lighthouse duties from vessel owners to help pay for its construction and maintenance. The lighthouse burned 213 gallons of whale oil annually, required 12 dozen wicks for its Argand lamps, 20 pounds of soap to clean its windows, 2 chamois skins to polish its reflectors and 10 pounds of whiting for painting its exterior.

John Chisholm, Collector of Customs, appointed William Nicholson as the keeper of the new lighthouse. He lived in the residence of the former dredge operator, McAffee, who had died of cholera in 1832. The new light could be seen 15 miles onto the lake.

Prosperity flourished at the canal until September 14, 1841, when a Select Committee was appointed to examine the manner of collecting customs and inquire into any abuses.

The committee found that collectors were not subject to local supervision, that their account books were considered private property, and that monetary returns were entirely unsatisfactory. The customs officers responded that their wages (5 percent of all tolls) were too small.

In England no two people from the same family were allowed to collect tolls, but at Burlington Bay nepotism ran wild. It was discovered that Collector of Customs at the canal, Wellington Square (Burlington) and Hamilton was John Chisholm, Sr. The deputy collector at the canal was his son John Chisholm, Jr. The deputy collectors at Wellington Square were yet another son of John Chisholm, Sr. and a Mr. Smith, son-in-law of John Chisholm, Sr. As well, the Collector of Customs at Oakville was John Chisholm, Sr.'s brother, William.

James Cull, Esquire, a civil engineer, gave further evidence that canal tolls and duties were mixed together so that neither could be accounted for. None of the Chisholms appeared before the committee, but John Chisholm, Sr. responded to written inquiries. When asked about annual receipts, he said he couldn't get the information without a great deal of trouble, and said he didn't know the number of vessels passing through the canal or their tonnage.

The government was furious and even began to survey a route for a new canal at Burlington Beach. However, the problem solved itself that very year with the failure of the Oakville Hydraulic Company owned by William Chisholm. The bank foreclosed on numerous Chisholm properties used as security in Wellington Square, Oakville and East Flamborough. The family lost prestige and John Chisholm, Sr. was replaced by John Davidson as Customs Collector at the canal.

It was also decided that the canal should be enlarged to 180 feet in width and deepened once again. Improvements continued in October 1842 with the construction of the Burlington Bay pier light, 14 feet above ground and wooden in construction. It had three Argand burners and three reflectors on an iron stand, and its fixed white light was visible four miles onto the lake.

During 1843 new piers were built, once again filled with stone secured by numerous stonehookers. A contract was also given to James Russell to obtain stone from a quarry 5½ miles distant on the mountain brow in Nelson Township. The quarry was located on the Clergy Reserves occupied by the Reverend Mr. Greene. To transport the stone a narrow-gauge railway was built. Cars were loaded at the quarry and sent down the track by gravitational force. The cars made a thunderous noise coming down the mountain, but speed slackened along the beach until the piers were reached. The empty cars were drawn back by horses.

Once the contract was complete, the entire railway plant of bridges, cars and rails was purchased by Andrew Miller of Hamilton and moved to a new site. This was the first railway built in the area of Wellington Square, and it is doubtful that better time has ever been made since by a train.

To further increase the breadth of the canal, ferry slips were built back into the piers and vessels no longer had to manoeuvre around the ferry scow. Also, an immense amount of dredging was done by two dredges, one horse-powered and the other propelled by steam.

By 1844 the canal improvements were complete, and because of easier access to the harbour a new steamer was built at the shipyard on the north neck of the beach. According to lightkeeper Thomas Campbell, Mr. Blannd built the wooden steamer *Britannia* and its launching was an important and exciting event on the beach, witnessed by many from Wellington Square. The *Britannia* was later rigged and outfitted as a top-sail schooner named the *Severn*, commanded by Captain Roberts. A few years later the shipyard was swept out of existence by yet another northeast gale and shipbuilding operations were shifted to Wellington Square.

In April 1846 a new lightkeeper came to the canal and stayed for the next 29 years. George

A top-sail schooner entering the Burlington Bay Canal.
(Oakville Historical Society)

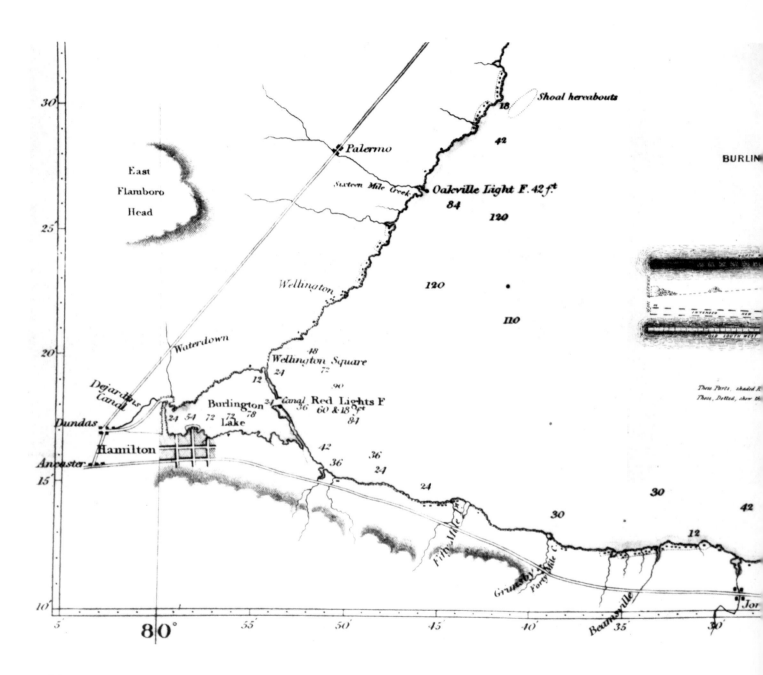

30'

East
Flamboro
Head

25'

20'

Dejardins
Canal

Dundas

Ancaster

Hamilton

15'

10'

5                    80°                    55'        50'              45'          40'        35'        30'

Shoal hereabouts

Palermo

18

42

Sixteen Mile Creek

Oakville Light F. 42 f.t

84

120

BURLIN

Wellington

120

110

Waterdown

48

Wellington Square

72

24

90

12

Burlington      24   Canal Red Lights F
Lake      78      36   60 & 18 f.t
24   54   72   72              84

42

36      36

24

24

30

30

42

12

Fifty Mile C.

Grimsby     Forty Mile C.

Beamsville     Jor

24

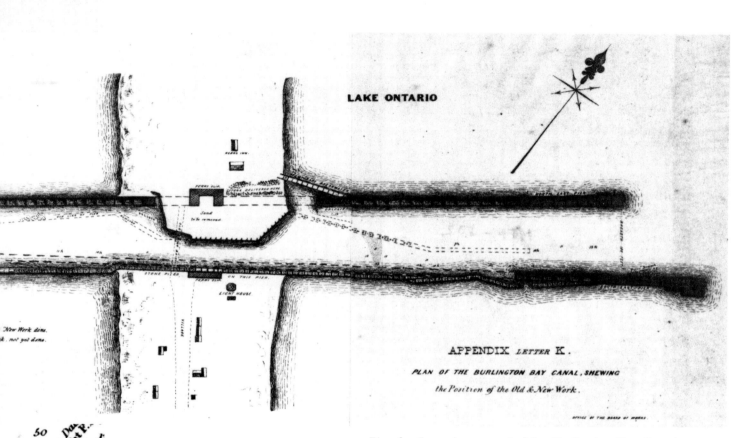

LAKE ONTARIO

APPENDIX LETTER K.

PLAN OF THE BURLINGTON BAY CANAL, SHEWING

the Position of the Old & New Work.

OFFICE OF THE BOARD OF WORKS

Plan for the enlargement of the Burlington Bay Canal dated 1845. (National Map Collection, Public Archives Collection)

Burlington Bay has carried a variety of names: Little Lake, Lake Geneva, Burlington Lake and Lake Macassa. In 1917 its name was changed to Hamilton Harbour.
(National Map Collection, Public Archives Canada)

Thompson was glad to get his feet back on dry land. Harrowing experiences on the lakes as mate of the schooner *Hamilton* had left their mark. When Customs Officer Davidson offered him the lightkeeper's position, he jumped at the chance.

Responsible for lighting the main light and pier-end lighthouse each sunset, he spent endless hours polishing reflectors, trimming wicks, and toting gallons of whale oil. The Argand lamps were found to be temperamental and it was hard to keep them lit during a gale, when their presence was essential. Thompson became ferryman as well, winching wagonloads of grain across the canal. The job was very demanding.

During the fall of 1848, at the height of a northeasterly gale, the barkentine *Ellenora* was seen approaching the canal, running before the wind. Waves were breaking over the piers and the pier-end light was obscured. The captain missed the canal entrance, and the *Ellenora* was driven into the north pier and was totally wrecked. Mr. Gage and Mr. Tallman salvaged what they could for the owners, but much of the merchandise was worthless. For some time after, steamers and schooners had to hug the other side of the canal to get past her. (50 years later, lightkeeper Captain Thomas Campbell reported that part of her keel and clamps were still observable.)

When the wind rose from the northeast, the worst place for a schooner to be was in the western end of Lake Ontario. Harbours of refuge were scarce and ships always faced the danger of grounding on the beach, or foundering if they attempted to ride out the storm anchored in the lake. Many ships went ashore on the beach during this period of sail, although they were often refloated, repaired and placed back into service.

For those vessels able to make the canal entrance, their problems were not over. Constant silting left many schooners stranded in the canal until a favourable wind piled enough water for them to make the passage. Crosscurrents at the entrance scraped many a vessel along the piers, and sparks from steamers often set the piers on fire, much to the consternation of the lightkeeper, who often had to rip up planking and throw it into the canal to put out the fires.

On July 18, 1856, one such disaster struck. Sparks from the government supply vessel, the steamer *Ranger*, bringing barrels of whale oil to the lighthouse, set the piers aflame. The fire began at 4 p.m. and spread rapidly, engulfing the main lighthouse, the pier light, the ferry house, the lightkeeper's house and Thompson's old dwelling house. Beach residents battled the flames for hours, but destruction was complete. Lightkeeper George Thompson spent the next few months in a shanty, his personal belongings and tools destroyed in the fire. It was a full 18 months before the piers and pier-end light could be rebuilt. A new brick lightkeeper's house (which still stands) was built in 1857 by contractor McCallum. The steamer *Ranger* had

The following is a partial list of vessels which ran into trouble at Burlington Beach from 1820 to 1867:

| Vessel | Type | Date | Fate |
|---|---|---|---|
| Wellington | Schooner | Nov. 21, 1820 | Wrecked |
| Union | Schooner | Sept. 24, 1825 | Aground |
| Commerce | Schooner | Nov. 1, 1831 | Aground |
| Rambler | Schooner | Nov. 1, 1831 | Aground |
| Elizabeth | Schooner | Fall, 1836 | Aground |
| Ellenora | Barkentine | Fall, 1848 | Wrecked |
| Henry Wheaton | Schooner | Apr. 15, 1854 | Aground |
| Emblem | Schooner | Apr. 15, 1855 | Aground |
| Ruby | Schooner | Aug. 9, 1855 | Aground |
| Queen Victoria | Schooner | Oct. 3, 1857 | Sunk (hit N.W. Pier) |
| Orion | Schooner | Oct. 2, 1859 | Aground |
| Berlin | Schooner | Nov. 10, 1860 | Aground |
| Admiral | Schooner | Oct. 4, 1861 | Aground |
| Hero | Tug | Aug. 28, 1863 | Aground |
| Peerless | Schooner | Oct. 31, 1863 | Hit pier and sunk |
| Linnie Powel | Schooner | Sept. 5, 1864 | Aground |
| Maggie | Schooner | Sept. 18, 1865 | Aground |
| Iris | Schooner | Sept. 1865 | Aground |
| Queen of Lakeshore | Schooner | May 4, 1867 | Aground |
| C.G. Alvord | Schooner | Dec. 13, 1867 | Wrecked |

The Burlington Bay lightkeeper's dwelling, built in 1857.
(Public Archives Canada, PA 46460)

The pier-end lighthouse, built in 1856. (Ontario Archives)

bad luck of her own. She was wrecked 10 years later at Port Stanley, in August 1866, after only 13 years of service on the Great Lakes.

The main lighthouse posed another problem. Public Works commissioners wanted a permanent stone lighthouse placed at the canal so that such a tragedy would never recur, and the search began for a qualified contractor with the skill and resources to complete such a task. The Public Works commissioners finally chose John Brown of Thorold to complete the project.

A Scot by birth, John Brown had emigrated to Canada in 1838. He opened quarries, plaster and cement mills, plaster beds, lime kilns and a steam sawmill. He also built scows, dredges and tugboats in his shipyards in Allanburgh and Port Robinson. As a contractor John Brown worked almost exclusively on government rail, canal and harbour contracts, and in 1857 had just completed the building of six limestone lighthouses known as the "Imperial Towers" on Lake Huron and Georgian Bay.

As a contractor, John Brown was highly regarded. His cement and plaster products won World Fair medals in Paris in 1855 and London in 1862, and John Brown was determined to uphold his good reputation when he undertook the building of the Burlington Bay lighthouse.

Work began on April 1, 1858, with the removal of the stone from the foundation of the old wooden lighthouse. Piles were driven, then levelled off and cross pieces of timber laid. This artificial foundation was bedded in concrete. The cellar walls were then constructed of limestone, fully 7 feet thick. These walls tapered and the thickness of the stone decreased as the tower rose, but the interior dimension remained constant. By the end of July, half of the lighthouse had been built and the schooner *Sardinia* arrived with the third and final load of stone from John Brown's quarry in Thorold.

Construction was not without attendant difficulties. John Brown's lifting scow was sunk during the first month of construction and another spring storm drove two more scows ashore in May. High water forced constant pumping of the cellar, the derrick of the schooner discharging stone was torn down by the vessel's main boom and, to top things off, a workman's horse jumped into the canal and had to be pulled out.

By September 1 the masons had completed the tower. All that remained was for the lantern room to be placed on top of the limestone and for the dome and copper cap to be fastened. As finishing touches, carpenters completed a beautiful spiral staircase, the lighthouse was painted white and the interior was whitewashed. It was John Brown's best work to date.

On the evening of October 18, 1858, two lamps with reflectors were lit in the lantern room — a beginning.

It was almost the end for lightkeeper Thompson because two weeks later one of the most terrible storms ever to hit the beach struck. Upon returning from lighting the pier-end lamp he was almost swept into the canal as waves broke over both sides of the pier. He

The Burlington Bay Imperial
light station, built in 1858 by
John Brown of Thorold.
(Hamilton Public Library)

Burlington Bay lighthouse keeper George Thompson. He served for 29 years (1846-1875). (Courtesy of Peter Coletti)

described the return trip as the most dangerous situation he had ever experienced. Drowning was a constant fear. Two of Thompson's ferrymen met that fate, and George Thompson himself came close a number of times after falling off the ferry scow.

Almost immediately the beautiful new lighthouse became embroiled in a bitter controversy which was to last over 20 years.

The new lighthouse and pier light were the first in Canada to be adapted to burn coal oil instead of whale oil. Mariners were furious. They felt that this new artificial fuel would deprive whalers of their livelihood and they lobbied heavily for the government to return to the use of whale oil. However, with the price of whale oil rapidly increasing and the supply uncertain, the government continued with their coal oil experiment, with such good results that by the 1860s many Canadian lighthouses converted to its use.

It took lightkeeper Thompson some time to adjust to these new lamps. They would smoke and choke themselves out. He also had a great deal of trouble warming the coal oil in cold weather. One December evening he wrapped the lamps with flannel and rope yarn. He kept the large light burning, but the coal oil partially froze. Thompson also experimented with a number of new lamps which were being introduced, some with glass tubes and some without, until he finally, grudgingly, gave coal oil his support.

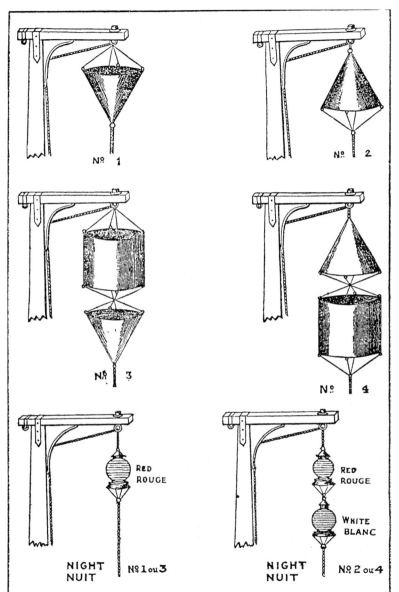

Nº 1

Nº 2

Nº 3

Nº 4

RED
ROUGE

RED
ROUGE

WHITE
BLANC

NIGHT
NUIT          Nº 1 ou 3

NIGHT
NUIT          Nº 2 ou 4

A 19th-century coal oil lamp and 180°
lens. (Canadian Coast Guard, Prescott)

Storm signals. The position and shape of these woven
baskets and lights warned mariners of approaching
gales.

33

A view of the ferry scow from the gallery of the lighthouse. (Hamilton Public Library)

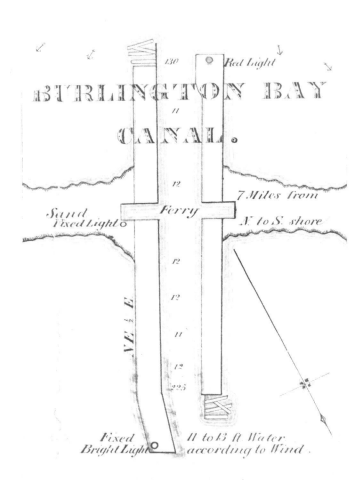

Map of the Burlington Bay Canal dated 1863.
(Ontario Archives)

Through it all, beach residents continued their fishing and subsistence farming (even though fishing with seines was no longer allowed in the bay); lightkeeper Thompson continued to growl at the ferry passengers and his neighbours; there were picnics on the beach in summer and team ice racing on the bay in winter; and vessels came and went.

From his new vantage point at the top of the stone lighthouse, George Thompson became a trained observer. In his lightkeeper's diary he noted the name of each vessel that came through the canal and he clocked the amount of time it took for a steamer to reach the canal from the moment he first heard the slap of its paddlewheels. (It took the steamer *America* 1 hour 23 minutes and the steamer *Spartan* 1 hour 16 minutes.) Thompson also noted the launching of many steam and sailing vessels at Hamilton and Wellington Square.

One such vessel was the schooner *Baltic*. She was launched May 6, 1867, at Wellington Square and immediately grounded. This was not a good beginning for a proud vessel which was to serve faithfully on the lakes for 27 years, until November 24, 1894. On a trip from Kingston to Oswego, New York, loaded with 12,600 bushels of wheat, the *Baltic*, with Captain Beard, his wife and three sons aboard, ran into a gale. With darkness coming on, the Captain attempted to enter Oswego harbour but was hit by a mountainous sea which knocked the *Baltic* out of control. Captain Beard began blowing distress signals and the lifesaving crew on shore got out the beach cart and followed the *Baltic* along the shore. The schooner fetched up, the lifesaving crew was able to get a line on her, and all hands were safely rescued. The following day the crew boarded the vessel and found the Beard family dog on top of a cupboard, a little wet and cold, but none the worse for his experience.

Another Wellington Square schooner, the *Azov*, bound from Meldrum Bay to Chatham on October 22, 1911, hit gale-force winds on Lake Huron and started to leak. Captain McDonald hoped to seek shelter at Harbour Beach, but time ran out. With the vessel sinking, the Captain hurriedly decided to abandon ship, sending his son, daughter and three crew members into the yawl before him. They had barely time to row clear before the *Azov* capsized.

Without provisions or protective rain gear the occupants of the yawl realized it would be impossible, because of the wind and sea, to reach the much closer American shore, so the decision was made to row for the Canadian side, taking advantage of the western wind. After 18 hours of bitter cold and rain, the yawl safely touched ground 6 miles north of Goderich with all hands saved.

Meanwhile the capsized *Azov*, because of her lumber cargo, retained enough buoyancy to continue drifting across Lake Huron. She finally fetched up on the shoals south of Chantry Island.

Over the years Captain McDonald maintained a warm affection for the yawl, keeping it freshly painted and in good repair.

Many area vessels from Hamilton, Dundas, and Wellington Square used the canal during lightkeeper Thompson's time. The following paragraphs describe but a few of these ships.

Making a number of trips early in 1854, the steamship *Royal* passed through the Burlington Canal delivering 11 locomotives to the Great Western Railway depot in Hamilton for the opening of the Toronto-Hamilton line. Three years later lightkeeper Thompson witnessed a rail disaster at the Desjardins Canal when one of the locomotives derailed. At 4:10 p.m., March 12, 1857, the locomotive *Oxford*, Hamilton-bound, derailed while crossing the swing bridge at Burlington Heights. Fifty-nine passengers and crew plunged to their deaths in the icy waters of the Desjardins Canal. It remains one of the worst rail disasters in Canadian history.

On July 22, 1854, at Hamilton, an attempt was made to launch the new sidewheel steamer *Europa*. The attempt failed and it was weeks before the *Europa* made her first recorded trip through the canal.

The Dundas steamer *Her Majesty* was too large to fit through the Welland Canal during the 1850s and was restricted to use on Lake Ontario.

On March 12, 1855, the steamer *Welland* picked up 120 barrels of whisky which had been delivered to the canal by sleighs crossing the bay.

The Wellington Square schooner *Baltic* lying wrecked on the beach at Oswego, New York, November 24, 1894.
(Ontario Archives)

The schooner *Azov* sailing through the Desjardins Canal.
(Ontario Archives)

Crew of the schooner *Azov*. (Ontario Archives)

The Dundas steamer (believed to be *Her Majesty*) in the
Dundas basin during the 1860s. (Ontario Archives)

The Hamilton-built steamer *Europa*.
(Public Archives Canada, PA 43035)

The steamer *Kingston* of the Royal Mail Line was a frequent visitor to the canal. She was built on the River Clyde in Scotland and shipped to Canada in pieces for assembly in Montreal. (Public Archives Canada, PA 136187)

The steamer *Kingston* of the Royal Mail Line, which visited Hamilton regularly in the 1850s, was prefabricated on the River Clyde in Scotland and shipped to Canada in pieces. The *Kingston* was assembled in Montreal and equipped with a large "walking beam" engine to power her paddlewheels.

On November 4, 1856, the brand-new piers at the canal were set on fire by the steamer *City of Hamilton*. This steamer began regular runs between Toronto and Hamilton on May 9, 1857.

While inspecting the schooner *Queen Victoria*, which had hit the piers and sunk on October 3, 1857, lightkeeper Thompson stopped to pick up 52 herring lying among the stones of the piers. His son collected 93 the next day.

After a heavy gale during the early years at the canal, herring could easily be picked up among the stones of the piers. (Joseph Brant Museum)

The schooner *Agnes* was exchanged for a Wellington Square house and lot on March 5, 1860.

On September 18, 1865, two schooners, the *Iris* and the *Maggie*, were driven ashore on Burlington Beach. It took two steamers, the *Wales* and the *Hercules*, to pull the *Maggie* off the sand, but the *Iris* had to be hauled onto the beach and rebuilt. She was relaunched on May 10, 1866. Word arrived six months later that the schooner *Iris* had gone to pieces at Port Hope.

The Wellington Square schooner *Baltic* had insult added to injury on November 27, 1894. Wrecked three days earlier at Oswego, New York, the grounded *Baltic* was hit and further damaged by the schooner *Daniel G. Fort*, which had also missed the harbour entrance.

The schooner *Gulnare*, which went ashore May 11, 1882, at Burlington Beach, was nicknamed "Bull of the Woods."

The schooner *P.E. Young*, dismasted by the canal railway bridge in 1891, was blown up as a public spectacle at the Canadian National Exhibition on July 1, 1898, when known as the U.S.S. *Maine*.

The schooner *Lillian*, one of the last surviving Lake Ontario stonehookers, ended her years as a boys' naval training vessel on Burlington Bay in 1929.

The steamer *City of Hamilton*, built in 1853 and owned at one time by John Proctor of Hamilton, was one of the infamous steamers to set fire to the piers at Burlington Bay Canal (1856). (Ontario Archives)

The schooner *Canadian* moored at the Burlington Canal. On June 8, 1874, the *Canadian* capsized six miles out and had to be towed into Bronte Harbour.
(Ontario Archives)

Early Hamilton paddlewheeler, the steamer *Argyle*.
(Hamilton Public Library)

The 400-ton steamer *Acadia*, launched at Hamilton on May 21, 1867, was the first vessel in Canada to be built on the composite principle. She had a steel hull and wooden upper decks. (Ontario Archives)

The schooner *Lillian* was one of the last "stonehookers" on Lake Ontario. She ended her years as a boys' naval training vessel on Burlington Bay. (Ontario Archives)

The schooner *Antelope*, built in 1854 by J.J. Abbey at Port Robinson. She was owned by Horn and Brothers of Hamilton. (Ontario Archives)

After 29 years of faithful service as lightkeeper at Burlington Bay, George Thompson retired. He cited reasons of poor health, from strenuous battles with the public and nature. As he departed the lighthouse en route to his farm in Millgrove, he took time to pause at Burlington Heights for a last look at the bay. He saw a new steamer leave its berth at Hamilton, go to the canal and return. That night in his diary George Thompson reminisced that the old steamer *Transit* never even left her wharf in that same amount of time.

Times had changed at the canal. Two large resorts, the Brant House and the Ocean House, were built on the beach in 1875, and traffic to the beach greatly increased. Competition between the two resorts was stiff. The Brant House offered easy access to sandy beaches and water sports. Acres of gardens and croquet and lawn bowling greens were also available. The Ocean House boasted a billiards room, a bar and a bowling alley. Both resorts had ballroom dancing and offered rail and water transportation to their front doors. (Mr. Benjamin Egar had a channel dug between Brant's Pond and Lake Ontario in 1875 to accommodate a small steam wherry which transported guests across the bay without going through the canal. The Department of Marine and Fisheries put an end to this unlawful channel shortly thereafter.)

The population on Burlington Beach boomed. "Villa" lots were sold for summer houses and a railway line was built along the beach. With the railway came a new influx of people, and the character of the beach changed. Fishermen and permanent residents gave way to seasonal visitors and picnickers. Roads were improved, as well. At the canal, schooners gave way to steamers and propellers were substituted for paddlewheelers. A fierce competition between railways and water transportation developed, which resulted in a great deal of litigation.

Vessel owners demanded that a new railway swing bridge remain open at all times, except when a train was crossing, and never be closed when a vessel was within one mile of the canal entrance.

However, on April 28, 1885, the bridge was slow to swing. The schooner *Lillie*, running to the harbour for shelter, was unable to stop and hit the railway bridge. She was dismasted and had her canvas torn.

Vessel owners again demanded the bridge remain open and added that tolls on ships going through the canal should be abolished since there were no tolls on the Welland Canal. Cries were also made for deepening the Burlington Bay canal to 12 feet.

The schooner *Northman*, out of Hamilton, was lost because of the continued shallowness of the canal. Caught in a northeast gale and knowing certain destruction awaited her at the canal, she had heaved to and foundered out in the lake. All hands were lost and marine factions wanted changes made.

The Lake Ontario pier during the 1880s. (Ontario Archives)

Proper attire for visiting the lighthouse. (Ontario Archives)

The Lakeside Hotel at the canal was originally built by Philip McGee during the 1830s and was known as the Ship's Inn. (Ontario Archives)

The Ocean House Resort on Burlington Beach, built in
1875. (Hamilton Public Library)

The Brant House Resort at Wellington Square.
(Joseph Brant Museum)

The north neck of the beach. (Hamilton Public Library)

Burlington Beach at the turn of the century.
(Hamilton Public Library)

The first locomotive to cross the new railway swing
bridge at the canal was engine *J.M. Williams*. It crossed
the canal from the north side on January 15, 1878.
(Hamilton Public Library)

Baxter's wharf at Wellington Square with bins of apples
ready for shipping. (Joseph Brant Museum)

The railway was warned not to interfere with canal traffic and for six years this arrangement proved satisfactory. Then, on August 30, 1891, at 11:40 p.m., a terrible accident occurred at the canal. The Grand Trunk freight train from Fort Erie, with engine, coal car, tender and nine box cars, arrived at the canal before the bridge could be swung closed. The train plunged into the canal, and fireman W.J. Couch and brakeman Robert Shaw were drowned. It took four weeks to remove the wreckage from the canal.

The railway once again began holding the bridge closed, and that same year, on December 6, the schooner *P.E. Young* ran into the railway bridge and lost her masts.

Tonnage and number of trips made by sailing and steam vessels through the Burlington Bay ship canal from July 1884 to June 1885 follow:

| Name of Sailing Vessel | Tonnage | Number of Trips |
| --- | --- | --- |
| Ella Murton | 229 | 34 |
| Undine | 196 | 32 |
| Olivia | 108 | 2 |
| Gulnare | 325 | 22 |
| Y.L. Wells | 76 | 2 |
| Erie Stewart | 230 | 6 |
| Elisa White | 128 | 4 |
| E.H. Rutherford | 286 | 16 |
| Mediterranean | 227 | 4 |
| Pride of America | 285 | 4 |
| Maggie McRae | 313 | 8 |
| E.R.C. Proctor | 162 | 14 |
| Bessie Berwick | 275 | 2 |
| Aurora | 234 | 4 |
| Accacia | 188 | 2 |
| Jessie McDonald | 84 | 2 |
| O. Mowatt | 295 | 4 |
| Cornelia | 95 | 2 |
| Gold Hunter | 219 | 2 |
| Defiance | 89 | 16 |
| Baltic | 164 | 2 |
| Kate Eccles | 121 | 2 |
| W.Y. Greenwood | 144 | 2 |
| Clara Youell | 269 | 2 |
| Speedwell | 181 | 6 |
| Julia | 107 | 8 |
| Craftsman | 278 | 2 |
| Erie Belle | 274 | 2 |
| Annandale | 180 | 4 |
| Hanlan | 107 | 2 |
| Flora Carretts | 190 | 2 |

| Name of Sailing Vessel | Tonnage | Number of Trips | Name of Steam Vessel | Tonnage | Number of Trips |
|---|---|---|---|---|---|
| Highland Beauty | 58 | 6 | Corinthian | 615 | 8 |
| W.W. Grant | 163 | 2 | Algerian | 576 | 10 |
| O.S. Storrs | 139 | 2 | Gen. Wolsley | 70 | 6 |
| E. Blake | 328 | 2 | Cuba | 599 | 2 |
| E.K. Hart | 86 | 2 | Clinton | 292 | 2 |
| North Star | 160 | 2 | California | 581 | 2 |
| Forest Queen | 137 | 2 | Canada | 408 | 6 |
| Herbert Dudley | 225 | 2 | Lake Michigan | 440 | 2 |
| Saint Louis | 333 | 2 | Acadia | 509 | 2 |
| Manzanilla | 320 | 6 | Augusta | 31 | 4 |
| Jesse H. Breck | 305 | 2 | Myles | 929 | 4 |
| Southampton | 319 | 2 | Canadian | 145 | 1 |
| Gaskin | 298 | 2 | Indian | 200 | 2 |
| Denmark | 305 | 2 | D.D. Calvin | 483 | 2 |
| Norway | 332 | 2 | M.R. Mitchell | 17 | 2 |
| Prussia | 376 | 2 | Lillie | 33 | 2 |
| Bavaria | 360 | 2 | Shickluna | 394 | 2 |
| St. Peter | 275 | 2 | C.J.S. Munroe | 31 | 2 |
| J.S. Richards | 259 | 2 | McArthur | 77 | 2 |
| G. Sherman | 307 | 2 | Lake Ontario | 412 | 28 |
| | | | Celtic | 440 | 32 |
| | | | Southern Belle | 264 | 4 |
| | | | Dominion | 376 | 24 |
| | | | Clara Louise | 14 | 2 |
| | | | Ontario | 92 | 2 |
| | | | St. Magnus | 541 | 6 |
| | | | Alma Munro | 581 | 12 |
| | | | Inez | 34 | 2 |
| | | | Corsican | 715 | 8 |
| | | | W.A. Booth | 32 | 2 |

There were tragedies at the canal, but also daring rescues. The new lightkeeper, Captain Thomas Campbell, by the turn of the century had saved 16 lives. On one occasion he rescued two men whose craft had capsized, pulling one man into the small lifesaving boat and lashing the other man to the stern and towing him to shore. (Captain Campbell had great diplomacy and tact. He named his lifeboats after the government officials who purchased them for him: Adam Brown and F. Goudreau.)

On another occasion, Dominion Day 1891, Captain Campbell jumped into the canal to save a young lady who had fallen out of a skiff. It was a hard struggle until assistance arrived, and Captain Campbell doubted he would have been able to manage had it not been for the 2,700 feet of lifesaving chain which lined the wall of the pier.

Captain Campbell was 60 years of age at the time and was already adorned with the Canadian Humane Association's medal for lifesaving. Captain Campbell saved lives, but on at least one occasion his own life was saved. On May 11, 1892, during a heavy northeast gale, the schooner *Gulnare* came to anchor half a mile south of the piers. Her deckload of tan bark and staves was washed ashore and no help could reach her. Captain Campbell went to light the pier light to guide her but was swept into the canal. He was rescued by a number of residents with a rope. The following day the vessel was able to heave to and come into the canal for repairs.

Because of the increased number of visitors to the canal, life lines were placed south of the canal for surf bathers and lifesaving balls with lines attached lined the piers. To aid mariners, three shoal buoys were provided as well as a storm drum signal station. The storm drums were large woven baskets hoisted from a mast to warn of approaching gales.

To provide entertainment at the canal, on October 31, 1891, the Royal Hamilton Yacht Club opened. Regattas soon drew even more people to the beach. Cottages sprung up and it was decided to replace the ferry service with a bridge across the canal. The old ferry scow was becoming more and more difficult to manage because of increased traffic and was deemed inappropriate and outdated. The ferryman was quick to agree because he never got a day off and Sundays were becoming his busiest days. A swing bridge across the canal was completed in 1896 but did not accommodate the public the way the old ferry had. The bridge was closed from 11 p.m. Saturday night until 6 a.m. Sunday morning, and many beachfront residents began complaining that their small boats would mysteriously "disappear," only to turn up on the other side of the canal the following morning.

The Royal Hamilton Yacht Club during the 1890s.
(Hamilton Public Library)

While trying to light up the pier-end lighthouse for the
schooner *Gulnare*, pictured here, lightkeeper Captain
Thomas Campbell was swept into the canal and had to
be rescued by a number of beach residents with a rope.
(Ontario Archives)

The steamer *Mazeppa* on Burlington Bay.
(Courtesy of Roger Chapman)

The small passenger steamer *Lillie*.
(Courtesy of Roger Chapman)

A busy day at the bayside piers.
(Public Archives Canada, PA C5112)

A rare photo of the steamer *White Star* at Brown's Wharf
(Port Flamboro). This area now houses the Lasalle Park
marina. (Courtesy of Roger Chapman)

The forces of nature were not kind to the new developments at the canal. Fire was a constant danger at the turn of the century. On July 17, 1895, the Ocean House and the Grand Trunk Pavilion burned down. The Yacht Club soon met the same fate. As well, sparks from steamers continued to set the piers afire, and on more than one occasion the services of a special train with the Hamilton Fire Brigade on board were requested by telegrams from Captain Campbell at the beach.

The piers were constantly being rebuilt every 10 to 15 years. Fire, accidents with vessels, and wave action made renewal of the wooden piers necessary. A series of April storms during the late 1800s swept away the wharves and pier lighthouses from Port Credit to Oakville and seriously damaged the pier-end lighthouse at Burlington. It had to be shortened as rotten timbers were removed and was eventually replaced by a white reinforced-concrete tower.

In 1905, after 30 years as lightkeeper, Captain Thomas Campbell retired. The beach had changed remarkably since his arrival. Long gone were the mysterious lights of the "wreckers" which lured unsuspecting vessels ashore on the beach, and the smugglers who had enjoyed an immunity from governmental control. Swamps had been filled in and sub-par land suddenly became desirable beachfront property.

A new era of heavy industrialization came to the area during the World Wars and lake freighters began replacing wooden steamers.

Hamilton even petitioned to have the name Burlington Bay changed to Hamilton Harbour. Passenger traffic on Lake Ontario was handled by ships such as the *Macassa*, *Modjeska* and *Northumberland*.

The entrance to the piers, however, remained treacherous. On October 1, 1945, the 60-foot ketch *Aggie* went aground at the Burlington Canal and became a total loss after being battered to pieces on the beach. The crew of the *Aggie* missed the channel and attempted to come about, but struck the sand bottom about 100 feet from shore. The seven crew members clung to the ketch for over an hour before help arrived. The *Aggie* had been built in 1888 by Captain James Andrew of Oakville and, having won 86 yachting championships, was the pride of that town.

Seven years later, on April 28, 1952, the 7,000-ton freighter, *W.E. Fitzgerald*, struck the north span of the bascule bridge, forcing beach traffic to be rerouted through Hamilton.

It was finally decided that the series of lights at the harbour entrance had to be changed to avoid confusion. The main limestone tower, built by John Brown in 1858, was removed from service in 1961 and the main light was placed at the top of the new lift bridge. A series of nine lights and buoys now guide ships safely through the canal.

The well-known Hamilton steamer S.S. *Macasa* on her
maiden voyage. (Courtesy of Roger Chapman)

S.S. *Modjeska* at Wabasso Park (Lasalle Park).
(Courtesy of Roger Chapman)

S.S. *Tubina* entering the harbour.
(Courtesy of Roger Chapman)

In 1909 the wooden pier-end lighthouse on the Lake
Ontario side was replaced with a concrete tower.
(Hamilton Public Library)

Picnics on the beach. (Hamilton Public Library)

An early bayside pier scene. (Hamilton Public Library)

With the advent of lift bridges at the canal came the
inevitable line-ups. (Hamilton Public Library)

Beach fashions. (Hamilton Public Library)

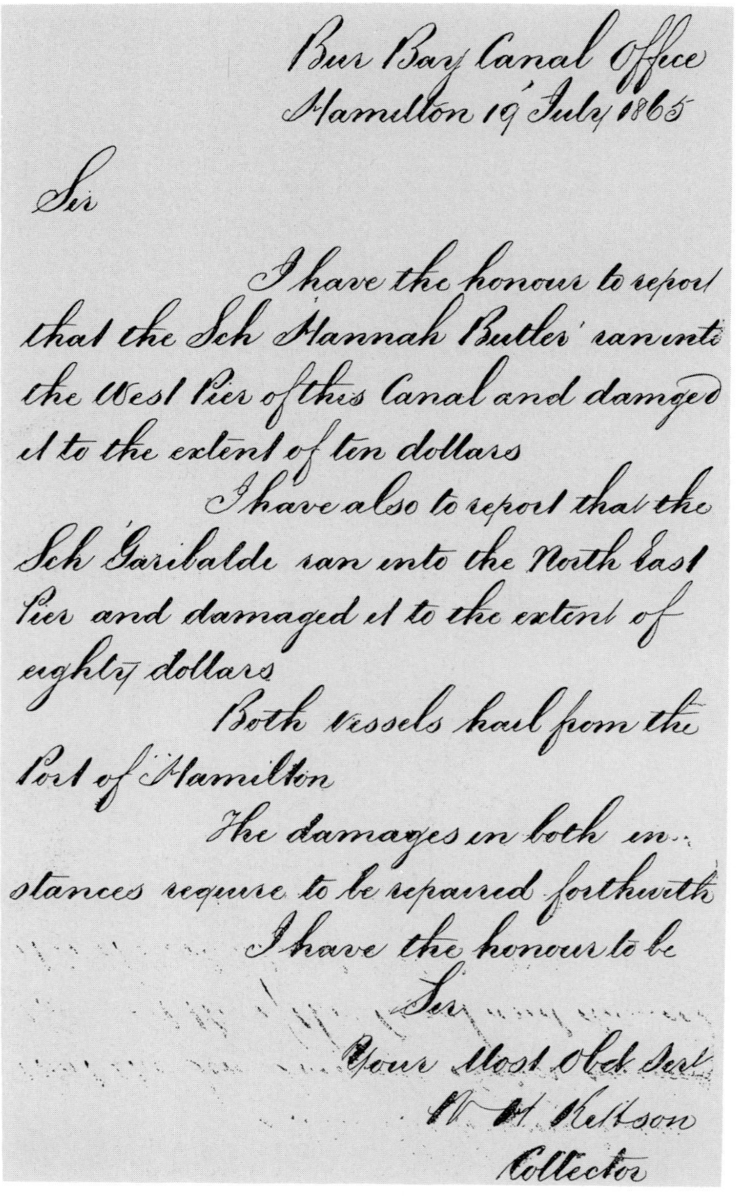

Bur Bay Canal Office
Hamilton 19 July 1865

Sir

I have the honour to report
that the Sch 'Hannah Butler' ran into
the West Pier of this Canal and damged
it to the extent of ten dollars

I have also to report that the
Sch 'Garibalde' ran into the North East
Pier and damaged it to the extent of
eighty dollars

Both vessels hail from the
Port of Hamilton

The damages in both in-
stances require to be repaired forthwith

I have the honour to be
Sir
Your Most Obdt Servt
W H Kittson
Collector

A damage report about early
schooners hitting the piers in
1865.

The damage report for the north span of the bascule bridge was slightly higher when the freighter *W.E. Fitzgerald* struck it on April 28, 1952. (Hamilton Public Library)

The first Burlington Bay skyway nearing completion in
1958. (Public Archives Canada, PA 138903)

Care of the lighthouse has remained a source of pride over the years. After Captain Campbell's retirement, a series of keepers attended the Burlington Bay light station, all exemplifying the qualities of self-reliance and individualism. They were Captain Thomas Lundy, Carl Van Cleaf, Bob Campbell, Harry Dunn, Mike Gushulak, Bill Lamb, and Peter Coletti.

George Thompson was an avid naturalist. He observed the habits of land tortoises or terrapins which nested near the lighthouse. He nursed back to health injured birds which had flown into the lantern room windows. Thompson also raised canaries.

George Thompson reported that the price of the Burlington stone lighthouse in 1858, including the foundation, superstructure, lantern room, lighting apparatus, and coal oil, was $10,479.98. His quarterly salary was $75.

Ghosts have haunted the lighthouse for years. Keeper Thompson, a spiritualist, often heard voices and noises coming from the stone lighthouse. Other keepers have spoken of footsteps and lights appearing in each consecutive window of the tower.

Captain Campbell was a beach historian. He wrote a series of articles about the beach for the Burlington *Gazette* in 1899.

When Captain Thomas Lundy took over as keeper in 1905, he was greeted by a new list of 104 rules for lighthouse keepers from the Deputy Minister of Marine and Fisheries.

Keeper Captain Thomas Lundy maintained that the stone for the foundation of the original wooden lighthouse had been brought to the canal as ballast from a number of early sailing vessels.

When builder John Brown died, he had contracts worth $2 million on the third Welland canal alone. He was a bachelor and left no will.

One keeper, who shall remain nameless, was a speed demon. He could race from the lighthouse to the local hotel, pour back two beers and be out the rear exit before his pursuing wife stormed through the front door.

Keeper Peter Coletti has continued the tradition of keeping birds as pets at the lighthouse. He has owned a series of budgies, finches, and African grey and Amazon green parrots.

Lightkeeper Coletti stated that many types of fuel have been used in the lighthouses over the years. Whale oil, coal oil, acetylene, petroleum vapours, and electricity have powered the lights. He also mentioned that the original lamp from the stone lighthouse now rests in the basement of the Joseph Brant Museum in Burlington.

Each keeper has spoken of the enjoyable experience of showing visitors through the lighthouse, sharing stories and warm feelings with those who have asked to see the light.

Mariners on the Great Lakes have never feared the "dangers of the deep." They were never happier than when there were many fathoms beneath their keel. It was only when they approached shore and potential safety that the perils of shoals and sand bars were realized.

The bayside pier lighthouse with Hamilton in the background.
(Canadian Coast Guard, Prescott)

Lighthouses and navigational aids have always served to guide them, and there was always a sense of security for sailors in knowing there was someone behind the light to aid them when they needed help. But lighthouses and keepers seem very remote from late-twentieth-century technology. Vessels are now guided by electronic computer and "Loran" systems, while navigational aids are controlled by light sensors and solar panels.

We must not forget, however, the power of the Great Lakes, with more dangers than any ocean, and the limestone tower beneath the twin skyways at Burlington Bay which serves as a monument to the hazards of the lakes.

The Burlington Bay light station was put out of service in 1961 but still stands today as a monument to those who have served "to keep the light." (Courtesy of Roger Chapman)

# BIBLIOGRAPHY

## BOOKS

Emery, Claire, and Barbara Ford. *From Pathway to Skyway — A History of Burlington*. Burlington, Ontario: Confederation Centennial Committee of Burlington, 1967.

*Historical Atlas of the Counties of Lincoln and Welland*. Toronto: Page, 1876.

Mansfield, J.B. *The History of the Great Lakes*. Toronto: J.H. Beers, 1899.

Metcalfe, Willis. *Canvas and Steam on Quinte Waters*. South Bay, Ontario: South Marysburgh Marine Society, 1979.

Thomas, Robert. *Register of the Shipping of the Lakes and River St. Lawrence*. Ontario: Wheeler, Mathews and Warren, 1864.

Wadsworth, J.J. *A Sketch of the Life and Work of Captain W.G. Miller*. Simcoe, Ontario: Norfolk Historical Society, 1902.

## NEWSPAPERS

Hamilton *Spectator* (1867)
Kingston *Chronicle* (1819-1820)
Niagara *Gleaner* (1824-1825)
Thorold *Post* (1876)
Toronto *Telegram* (1937). C.H.J. Snider, Schooner Days Series.

## FILES, PAPERS, REPORTS

Joseph Brant Museum files, including the diaries of George Thompson (1854-1875) and the Ghent papers

Burlington Historical Society files

Canada Sessional Papers
Department of Marine and Fisheries, annual reports, 1867-1920
Department of Railways and Canals, annual reports, 1875-1900
Department of Public Works, annual reports, 1855-1860

House of Assembly journals, annual reports of the Burlington Bay Canal Commissioners, 1825-1841